Creative Juices Publishing

Made in the USA
Monee, IL
14 October 2022

15874849R00063